FOR

I THINK YOU'D ENJOY THIS BOOK BECAUSE

FROM

PRINCIPLES FOR THE NEXT CENTURY OF WORK

Sense & Respond Press publishes short, beautiful, actionable books on topics related to innovation, digital transformation, product management, and design. Our readers are smart, busy, practical innovators. Our authors are experts working in the fields they write about.

The goal of every book in our series is to solve a real-world problem for our readers. Whether that be understanding a complex and emerging topic, or something as concrete (and difficult) as hiring innovation leaders, our books help working professionals get better at their jobs, quickly.

Jeff Gothelf & Josh Seiden

Series co-editors **Jeff Gothelf** and **Josh Seiden** wrote *Lean UX* (O'Reilly) and *Sense & Respond* (Harvard Business Review Press) together. They were co-founding principals of Neo Innovation (sold to Pivotal Labs) in New York City and helped build it into one of the most recognized brands in modern product strategy, development, and design. In 2017 they were short-listed for the Thinkers50 award for their contributions to innovation leadership. Learn more about Jeff and Josh at www.jeffgothelf.com and www.joshseiden.com.

OTHER BOOKS FROM SENSE & RESPOND PRESS

Lean vs. Agile vs. Design Thinking
What you really need to know to build
high-performing digital product teams
Jeff Gothelf

Making Progress
The 7 responsibilities of the innovation leader
Ryan Jacoby

Hire Women
An Agile framework for hiring and retaining women in technology
Debbie Madden

Hiring for the Innovation Economy
Three steps to improve performance and diversity
Nicole Rufuku

Lateral Leadership
A practical guide for Agile product managers
Tim Herbig

The Invisible Leader
Facilitation secrets for catalyzing change,
cultivating innovation, and commanding results
Elena Astilleros

What CEOs Need to Know About Design
A business leader's guide to working with designers
Audrey Crane

The Government Fix
How to innovate in government
Hana Schank & Sara Hudson

Outcomes Over Output
Why customer behavior is the key metric for business success
Josh Seiden

OKRs at the Center
How to use goals to drive ongoing change and
create the organization you want
Natalia Hellesoe & Sonja Mewes

What Do We Do Now?
A product manager's guide to strategy in the time of crisis
Randy Silver

Ethical Product Development
Practical techniques to apply across
the product development life cycle
Pavini Reddy

Hiring Product Managers
Using Product EQ to go beyond culture and skills
Kate Leto

To keep up with new releases or submit book ideas to the press, check out our website at www.senseandrespondpress.com.

THE CULTURE PROJECT

Copyright © 2020 by Thomas Bradbury

All rights reserved. No part of this publication may be reproduced, stored in a retrieval system, or transmitted, in any form or by any means, electronic, mechanical, photocopying, recording, or otherwise, without the prior written permission of the publisher.

Issued in print and electronic formats.
ISBN 979-8-5584238-4-6 (KDP paperback).

Editor: Victoria Olsen
Designer: Mimi O Chun
Interior typesetting: Jennifer Blais

Published in the United States by Sense & Respond Press
www.senseandrespondpress.com

Printed and bound in the United States.
1 2 3 4   23 22 21 20

Thomas Bradbury

THE CULTURE PROJECT

30 Days to Reboot Your Organization

INTRODUCTION

My work as an entrepreneur for over two decades has focused largely on corporate transition and transformation. The second business that I started, which I sold at the end of 2017, designed connectivity, infrastructure, and systems for voice, data, and collaboration whenever a corporation would invest tens of millions of dollars to design and build a new workplace.

It required us to understand every aspect of technology that the client was currently using as well as what they were considering for the future. It was astounding to witness the friction and poor decision-making associated with this process—even with some of the most globally renowned brands. Nowhere was there conversation that considered talent and technology together to support productivity and value. The inefficiencies and watered-down outcomes that inevitably developed captured my attention.

As I dug deeper to understand just how to help these corporate machines evolve their approach to this process, I would find time and time again that this issue of looking at talent and technology separately was not specific to building a new workplace. It became evident that corporate silos and departmental agendas drove decision-making that prioritized operational goals over ones centered on productivity and value. And in these times driven by the consumerization of technology and employee-centric programs, too many corporations were just "not getting it."

This became the mission and focus for my next venture. I developed a methodology for assessing the nexus between talent and technology. I was engaged to assess all types of businesses across North America—large Fortune 500 global brands, midsize private businesses, small sophisticated entities, and everything in between. What I often witnessed was straight out of a satirical comedy about the workplace: Band-Aids over laptop cameras for fear of being watched, sensitive client loan information forwarded to personal Google accounts for easier collaboration with coworkers, reserved but empty conference rooms driving real estate "requirements" and/or the construction of new meeting spaces, ineffective working-from-home policies leading to personal email communication with a client that became unexpected evidence in a costly litigation battle over a failed project, large numbers of employees leaving to go to a local deli for long lunches and coffee breaks because of better Wi-Fi coverage for their personal devices, newly hired employees waiting two weeks for their computers and email address, IT (information technology) departments with a plan to move to the cloud six months *after* the move into a new $100 million workplace, IT cost-cutting measures lowering the bar for information security shortly before a ransomware attack, employees continually being asked to travel cross-country to clients who would prefer virtual training sessions, highly compensated teams constantly spending weeks building content and proposals that already exists somewhere across the organization's network... I literally can provide hundreds of examples that are devastatingly impactful to technology ROI (return on investment), employee engagement, knowledge-worker productivity, and, ultimately, the bottom line.

I've spent these last few years trying to find the stakeholders within these businesses that could help me make a difference. And while we've had some degree of success working through various stakeholders, it is crystal clear that the common denominator for profound and lasting progress around culture, talent, and technology is getting leadership to not only buy in to these fundamental initiatives but also to lead the charge. This book walks you through exactly how to do that. It details the hard work, discomfort, and leadership needed to build the foundation of your organization's culture by aligning your talent and technology.

Some might ask how using this book to align talent and technology impacts your organization's culture. In 2006, Davide Ravasi and Majken Schultz wrote in their Academy of Management article "Responding to Organizational Identity Threats: Exploring the Role of Organizational Culture" that they:

> "broadly define organizational culture as a set of shared mental assumptions that guide interpretation and action in organizations by defining appropriate behavior for various situations. These largely tacit assumptions and beliefs are expressed and manifested in a web of formal and informal practices and of visual, verbal, and material artifacts, which represent the most visible, tangible, and audible elements of the culture of an organization."

Getting to the very heart of how, why, and when people within your organization communicate, collaborate, and produce will attack assumptions, situational behaviors, conflicting modes of operation, and more. And though I acknowledge that there are other factors and inputs to an organization's culture (such as history and risk preferences), using the alignment of talent and technology not only provides a universal vehicle in which to structure your initiative, but it also provides objective and tangible reference points for new and better outcomes.

And again, I can't state this enough: If the leader enacts this change themselves, that alone brings about positive cultural change.

For a leader to confront these foundational flaws across the organization, it means spending time understanding the day-to-day realities of how people work. And admittedly, doing this work will, for a certain amount of time, take them away from other very important parts of their job description. This was a very serious consideration when writing this book. That is exactly why "The Culture Project" is a decisive action plan for rapid change. One that can be absorbed and executed in a single month. Think of it as a field manual for breaking through the issues and obstacles that destroy or damage cultures—in a decisive and expeditious manner.

It provides "startup" energy for a corporate leader to leverage while immersing themselves in "the weeds" for a finite period of time to directly challenge what has been the regular flow and sequencing of thoughts, ideas, and actions.

While reading this book, I ask you to keep the following considerations in mind:

» Scheduling and implementing the work described in this book in 30 contiguous days might be challenging. In fact, for some firms, it might not be the best course of action. What is important about the 30 days is that the leader takes responsibility for this work themselves. Knowing that this leader has bigger strategic initiatives to focus on *and* that the work in this book is in the weeds, we need to program it in such a way that leaders will be able to see a start and end to their time in the weeds. Because, as important as it is to get a leader focused on this work, it's equally as important to establish this new foundation and allow the leader to float back to the helm of the business and continue the important leadership role in a macro sense.

» The Culture Project was written not only for current CEOs. It was written for other C-level executives as well as for aspiring leaders working their way up through the ranks, shaping their perspectives and preparing to take the next step in their career.

» The Culture Project leads a horse to water. The nature of this work means that for any leader to follow through with what is right for the business, the problems and needs for new policies and solutions become self-evident. Resetting the culture of an organization is no easy task. However, if used properly, this book positions a leader to witness the underbelly of the business they run.

» The Culture Project was completed before the COVID-19 pandemic. What's interesting is that the pandemic offers leaders a unique opportunity to seek (or maybe even demand) a new model for tech and talent alignment. This "black swan" event gives them the opportunity to cut through their own organization's bureaucracy. The urgency to find efficiencies offers leaders the chance to move ineffective people to the side and commit to this new model. Essentially, this time offers businesses an amazing window to reset their organization's culture around the alignment of talent and technology.

Here are some common attributes of an organization that is sorely in need of the work detailed in this book:

» You recognize that the business looks at IT as a service and support center.
» Your CIO (chief information officer) was hired for their operational prowess.
» HR (human resources) is not involved in growing and tracking digital adoption.
» Employees constantly leverage personal apps and tools to get their work done rather than the corporate IT solutions provided them (aka shadow IT).
» Your CIO does not have standing check-in meetings (monthly or quarterly) with senior executives and line-of-business managers.
» Infosec is constantly referenced as a reason to withdraw consideration of new platforms and solutions.

- » Infosec is part of IT, not a separate group reporting to the business and legal department.
- » Glassdoor reviews are littered with negative comments around outdated technology and/or general comments about the company being stuck in the past.
- » Employees consistently complain about meeting space availability.
- » Working from home is inefficient or even ineffective.
- » The firm has not embraced cloud computing.
- » The firm has not embraced Big Data or Artificial Intelligence.

Also, keep in mind the three phases of this work:
- » *Take Notice*: You need to see what's going on yourself!
- » *Activate:* Introduce fresh ideas and new models and implement them!
- » *Convert:* Make it happen!

Finally, remember that the Culture Project can be launched at any time. However, keep in mind that there are specific catalyst events throughout the corporate lifecycle that serve as triggers providing both opportunity for serious traction as well as significant risk if we don't shape informed investments in the firm's future. Here are examples of these costly and complex events:
- » A merger or acquisition
- » The hiring of a new leadership team
- » A founder-to-successor leadership transition within a family-owned business
- » A corporate workplace relocation or renovation
- » Recovery from an information security event
- » A black swan scenario—a pandemic, major weather event, major economic event, etc.

On the pages that follow, you will gain insights for each of the next 30 days that connect directly to the prescribed reflection or actions. You'll need to trust your instincts as you toggle between leading change yourself and catalyzing others to forge new conditions and relationships. Together, you and your team can follow through with the work outlined in this book to reset your organization and cultivate a new and stronger culture with a foundation that has your talent and technology aligned.

And this foundation will adapt to and support strategic plans moving forward including initiatives for artificial intelligence/machine learning/automation, your real estate strategy, talent attraction and retention, a raised awareness of infosecurity, higher levels of employee engagement, and, of course, increased productivity and value. The results will be a more engaged, productive, and valuable organization.

Enjoy rolling up your sleeves and making a difference. Let's get started.

PHASE I:
TAKE NOTICE

DAY 1: WHAT'S BOTHERING YOU?

Why did you pick up this book? What are you hoping to read, learn, or trigger? Do you feel like things are stale? Are you not the same leader you were a handful of years ago? Like many others, you may have become complacent. And although you try to focus on the big picture as is standard for an executive, you also have those wheels turning in the back of your mind. That's where you push the little thoughts driven by gut-level instinct. And you suppress them. Why? Because you see the silliness around you. You see the inefficiencies, waste, mediocrity, and lack of innovation. You keep your objective thoughts and observations to yourself.

Because confronting those thoughts and objectively taking action is not easy. You can't be on autopilot as a leader and expect your business and people to evolve. If you haven't been willing to get your hands dirty and do the right things for the business, perhaps that's why you cracked open this book.
So, do you want the good news or the bad news first?

The bad news is that it's not going to be easy. In fact, it will be uncomfortable at times. I'm guessing that you can think back to moments from earlier in your career as you grew into a leader and dealt with this discomfort. Striking down the bullshit, having difficult conversations, making decisions that you have been avoiding because they were in the weeds and left for others to deal with; this is how you'll be confronting the status quo.

You know what the good news is? You are no dummy. As a leader, you understand that nothing worthwhile is easy. And taking on this 30-day project is just that. The hard stuff that brings about the good stuff. And your Day 1 is coming to terms with being outed. Outed as a leader who has become complacent and allowed the business to devolve into something that you are not proud of. Let's grab it by the horns over the next 30 days and breathe life into something that you will once again be proud of. And that will turn into something that's amazing for everyone. And that's being a real leader. Being able to identify where the changes need to be made and then *willing* to make those changes for the benefit of everyone—even when those beneficiaries come along for the ride kicking and screaming.

TODAY

Write this stuff down. Just get a notebook, open a Word doc, dictate to Alexa... whatever it takes. Just start to cough up all the stuff that needs to be addressed. It's cathartic and it will set you on a path to lead again. The Culture Project is about building a ramp over the next 30 days that sets your business up to take flight and change the trajectory of your journey.

DAY 2: ACKNOWLEDGE THAT THE LANDSCAPE HAS CHANGED

Technology has changed everything.

And this sweeping change has challenged almost every tenet of work—employees, the physical workplace, innovation, and leadership. We are sleeping, traveling, and on vacation while information keeps flowing to our devices. And when we are at work, we often have little time to do actual, meaningful, and satisfying work because we are too busy meeting and talking about doing work.

Businesses want their employees to be reliable, conscientious, respectful, hard-working, smart, innovative, caring, knowing, creative, analytical, productive, and efficient. We've always wanted these attributes in the people we associate with and rely upon. But now there's a difference: We *need* it in a working environment that is changing daily as we sprint toward the future.

In any business, we need people who care. People who are employees who care about doing the right thing, care and respect their colleagues and managers, care about the quality of the products and services, care about the clients they serve, and, of course, care about the bottom line. We want our employees to solve problems, come up with ideas for new and improved products, let us know when something is not happening in a productive or effective manner, and represent us well. Anything else can be a huge liability. People who aren't representative of what we want out of our business bring others down, lower expectations, increase mediocrity, and drag down profits.

Why am I telling you this? It's likely that the last few paragraphs are not informing you of anything you don't already know. And it all makes complete sense to you. Of course, that's what businesses and leadership want! But is that what you have? And I mean really, truly have?

TODAY

Make two lists. It's crucial that you are brutally honest with yourself when you make both of these lists. If it makes you feel better, I'm not going to ask you to show anyone either of these lists. They will be your secrets. Hopefully, this will allow you to be as honest with yourself as possible because the more you can do that, the more impact this will have on reenergizing your desire and ability to lead.

For the first list, write down eight to 10 initiatives that are happening in your company right now that are meaningful and satisfying. Next to each of these 10 initiatives, write the names of those people associated with it that are the types of employees that your business wants and needs.

For the second list, write down eight to 10 initiatives that are happening in your company right now that you know as a leader are *not* meaningful nor satisfying. Next to each of these lousy initiatives, write the names of those people associated with it that are *not* currently exhibiting attributes that your business wants and needs.

Tuck away these two lists so that you can reference them in the coming days and weeks.

DAY 3: ESTABLISHING URGENCY STARTS WITH YOU

Are you ready? Because we start whenever you, the leader, are ready to identify the roadblocks in your organization.

The Culture Project needs to be addressed by a leader with a macro perspective of the business. A leader willing and capable of looking at the org chart from above and laying over it a detailed plan for moving the business forward. It needs to be charted in a way that brings everyone together to do their part in conjunction with others to produce the whole.

Now, what if you put just one of these groups or departments in charge of this initiative? What type of approach would be required to rise above their day-to-day agenda to get all stakeholders to work toward a common goal?

The leader must demand collaboration. In the corporate environment, this is often seen as a risk. Competing silos might not believe in the initiative and seek to sabotage it. Why? Because you are asking executives—that very well might have been playing the corporate game their entire careers—to act like entrepreneurs.

It's difficult enough getting someone to rise above their own agenda. To then get a group of corporate executives to be entrepreneurs… well, that might be near impossible. So, what does an organization do? Simple. A strong leader acts and rallies the team. When you peel back the various initiatives and follow the trail of accountability, they all lead to the main artery of the business. And the only person that is central enough to see this and be this is the leader: you.

TODAY

Construct a list of five initiatives that you have expressly delegated to departmental leaders and reflect on them. Here's what you should consider.

- » Did you get the results that you projected when you assigned each leader the initiative?
- » Do you recall a gut feeling sensing the initiative was getting watered down?
- » Did you accommodate watered-down results out of concern that you'd have to get in the weeds to fix it?
- » Did the results of any of these initiatives line up with the respective strategy that you were presented for approval?

You may see some overlap with the lists you prepared on Day 2. However, today's list is more about contemplating the mechanics of how you have been delegating, reviewing, approving, and holding others accountable. This will allow you to map what you see and hear over the next 27 days back to the original expectations and how they may have become corrupted along the way.

DAY 4:
BE PREPARED FOR PUSHBACK

There's nothing that elicits more apprehension than an announcement at work that there are changes afoot. Layoffs? A new boss? More paperwork? Longer hours? Different role? A new system to learn? Some of us are going to work from home permanently?

No matter how positive the changes might be, the natural human instinct is to panic: "What does this mean for me?" Accordingly, it's no small endeavor to impact the culture of your business. Knowing employees will instinctively put up their guard, you must be prepared for resistance: Employees want a sense of security and comfort. Without it, they become uncomfortable, insecure, sensitive, and defensive.

Exacerbating this drag on progress is what we went through in Day 3; the tendency to delegate culture matters to HR and other departments. These departmental leaders are typically not seen or positioned to allay this fear and discomfort. As you think this through today, you will quickly see and feel the importance of chairing The Culture Project yourself during these first 30 days.

In three weeks, you'll be addressing the changes transparently, letting everyone know specifically what you are doing, how you are positioning the firm's future, and, of course, *why* you are embarking on The Culture Project. Defining all of this is not today's concern. However, before doing so, you will encounter many uncomfortable leaders and employees. It's important to move forward knowing what's to come.

TODAY

As you prepare to roll up your sleeves and engage in areas of the business that you have typically delegated to others, start to write down exactly what you'll want to tell them about what you're doing. So how do I suggest you do this? Simply tell people exactly what you would want to know if you were in their position. Here are some specific thoughts and ideas on what that might be.

- » What exactly is The Culture Project and how can employees learn about it?
- » What made you feel as though you needed to make these changes?
- » How will The Culture Project have a positive impact on my job, career, and life?
- » What can employees expect to encounter along the way?
- » Will there be new and improved support for employees?
- » How long will it take?
- » Why will The Culture Project be different from past initiatives that were billed as good for everyone but didn't really pan out to be so?

Now that you have a clear view of how you'll address employees and leaders both throughout the process and then again during a milestone communication on Day 25, you are well positioned for Day 5. It is here that we will examine a rarely recognized breakdown in communication, collaboration, and productivity that corrupts a business culture and limits the future. And this is where we find the obstacle that must be confronted head-on during The Culture Project.

DAY 5:
FOCUS ON TALENT PLUS TECH

Every business invests in two primary assets: talent and technology.

Senior management is continuously seeking to raise the bar on the quality and performance of both. They are fully aware that these are the dual elements of the company's very DNA.

However, investing in talent and technology is simply the starting point. Leveraging them as a driving force comes only when they are structured to work in tandem. The problem is, talent and technology tend to sit in discrete silos. This will be our focus. This will be our vehicle for attacking the legacy culture. You must identify specific areas in which talent is unable to leverage tech to access people and data in order to get ROI on the business' most important investments. By examining this nexus, we will clearly see the impact to the business while simultaneously making self-evident the opportunities to invest and merge the talent and technology into a seamless force that generates maximum productivity.

I'm sure there are significant efforts in your business for initiatives around big data, machine learning, business intelligence, automation, etc. This is important work as you seek to accomplish new objectives such as innovating your products and services or leveraging data across multiple platforms for new insights and perspectives. But, how many of these efforts include or are focused on integrating your talent with these and other technology tools and applications? This is very important to note because only the top-layer concepts and benefits of all new transformative initiatives are presented to you. While there's a ton of value to be had, the ROI in most cases will rely on your talent and this is exactly the domain we will focus on.

TODAY

You will focus on two things.

First, look back on the significant technology transformational efforts that have been presented to you over the past 12 to 18 months.

> » What were the goals and objectives?
> » What were some of the actions associated with the planning and rolling out of such initiatives?
> » Who was leading each respective project?

Secondly, consider the people (users) and how their perspectives will drive the success of such business initiatives.

> » To what kind of users will these tech-based initiatives cater?
> » What kind of users might such initiatives challenge?
> » Does an environment currently exist within your organization to support all of these people?
> » What comes to mind as you map these initiatives to both existing and future employees?

It's highly likely that the initiatives you look back on today, Day 5, may also be on your list of meaningful and satisfying projects from Day 2 or projects that you delegated to others on Day 3. This progression in how you think of past and current initiatives now allows you to begin to develop questions in your own mind specifically for how investments in technology traditionally take shape throughout the business. This will position you well to see and understand exactly what needs to be addressed differently in the coming days.

DAY 6: TAKE STOCK OF YOUR TEAM'S LEGACY LENS

Who do you have around you? Are your deputies and lieutenants silo enablers? Or do they have a track record of seeking genuine collaboration from other silo leaders to help bring about outcomes that benefit the business holistically?

It's important to remember that we aren't looking to measure things the way we've always measured them. We aren't looking for people to stay in their respective lanes. We need leaders that are willing to move outside of their comfort zone and help challenge the status quo.

Look carefully at your team. Who do you bring into your immediate discussions? And which other senior people can be valuable once a bit of momentum is achieved? Be wary of those that will consciously or subconsciously thwart your efforts to improve. They are frightened and don't want to have their comfort zones challenged. Their infiltration into The Culture Project will sometimes threaten to sabotage your intentions and plans. Be keenly aware of any "malicious compliance," in which cunning executives purposely follow your guidelines in a way that they know will not meet the intended results.

TODAY

Spend 30 to 45 minutes meeting with each member of your leadership team. Reference your two lists of 10 current initiatives and the people associated with each of them before your meetings. Here's what you should think through as you further reflect on your work from Day 2.

> » Which senior leaders or key departmental stakeholders were on each of those respective lists?
> » Now that you have commenced The Culture Project, have you reshaped your perspective around what you initially listed as a meaningful or satisfying initiative?
> » Would you add or remove anyone associated with the initiatives on either of these lists?
> » What patterns of stakeholder involvement can you identify?
> » Is there any indication within those patterns that stand out as evidence to support key people who should be involved early in The Culture Project?
> » Do you observe any patterns within these lists from Day 2 that is making your gut tell you to hold off on involving certain key people until more groundwork is established as part of The Culture Project?

True leaders not only think more than two steps ahead, but they can also sort their thinking into "today" and "tomorrow." They can transcend the practical reality of what must happen today to continue doing business and think about how we can be more successful, efficient, and profitable in the future. Bottom line: They can call a timeout from tactical thinking and spend time thinking strategically about tomorrow.

DAY 7: BUILD AND COMMIT TO YOUR STRIKE FORCE

As the leader, you know that change must occur, and that it must start with you. In fact, for many organizations, failure occurs precisely because leaders are unwilling to innovate or disrupt their own way of thinking. The old line about insanity being defined as doing the same thing over and over while expecting different results comes to mind.

The most effective way to reconfigure your approach is to compartmentalize your time. By setting aside time each week, you'll be able to step outside of the organization's "bubble" and think with greater insight and clarity. Accordingly, you need a group of like-minded colleagues with you every step of the way.

I like to call this group your "Strike Force." The moniker Strike Force denotes urgency and precision.

And while you have a Strike Force, it doesn't diminish the role of the leader. Why do I say this? Because it's imperative to have a strong leader to function as judge and jury so that "designed by committee" and other attributes of the current legacy culture don't corrupt the "true north" of the mission. You'll rely on the Strike Force to offer insights and observations about not only the business and culture, but also about you, the leader, when you aren't walking the walk yourself.

Partitioning your time to leverage the Strike Force members both individually and collectively generates a constant workstream that sits outside of the day-to-day grind allowing space for innovative thinking. For example, at one of my companies I pushed myself to create a Strike Force when I sensed the need for a shift in thinking to not only address challenges and opportunities in the marketplace but also to collaborate on problem-solving. By selecting excellent advisors, and using their time effectively, it allowed me to grow, learn, and change in ways that brought benefits I could never have imagined.

TODAY

Think through the patterns of your typical week. Look at your schedule and ask the following questions.
- » What meetings are scheduled throughout your typical week?
- » Are all of these meetings important?
- » Are you getting meaningful work done with colleagues?
- » Which ones are unproductive and uninspiring?
- » How can you challenge yourself to really rethink and reshape your week in general?

What's most important today is that you commit to the scheduling of the Strike Force meetings as well as to the ancillary meetings and interviews that will be required for The Culture Project over the 23 days ahead. While it would be great to devote 100 percent of your time to The Culture Project, it's not realistic. As a leader, you will have to give attention to the day-to-day business activity. You must compartmentalize your time accordingly and set yourself up for success with The Culture Project.

DAY 8: SET EXPECTATIONS FOR YOUR STRIKE FORCE

How many people should be on your Strike Force? I recommend at least five and no more than seven. We want enough people to generate thought leadership, but not too many that the Strike Force becomes a mini bureaucracy. Assembling this group and getting off to a strong start is paramount. A cadence of two meetings a week out of the gate to plan early steps is the right move. Once individual members start to chair initiatives, meeting once a week will suffice for updates and the opportunity to collaborate or use others as a sounding board.

By setting the tone immediately, you will create the psychological safety for free thinking and authenticity. You need to encourage ideas that run against the grain of the legacy perspective. At first, it might be a bit difficult to evolve ideas that don't sound familiar. It is common for this to happen. Before you and your Strike Force untether yourselves from the thinking of the existing day-to-day realities, you'll find yourselves expressing thoughts and ideas within the confines of how things are currently done, how certain leaders within the organization think and approach their work, any current limitations with technology, or a general sense of what you think will be accepted by employees at large.

TODAY

Prepare for the next five days of identifying and approaching future members of your Strike Force. You must define, in your own mind, how you will approach these worthy and valuable colleagues. When you meet with them, you'll need to be direct and emphatic. Here are some suggestions:

> » Be ready to describe The Culture Project and why it's important for the business.
> » Order more copies of this book to hand out to each member to read with urgency.
> » You must be prepared to let them know that you mean business. Make a statement about how this work to improve the business and the associated changes are not optional. Future statements and actions over these 30 days will illustrate your unwavering commitment to the organization.
> » Be direct by letting them know you'll be challenging them and that they'll need to challenge you

(respectfully, of course).
- » You must be extremely clear when you inform them that by accepting the invitation to join the Strike Force, they must compartmentalize this work you are doing together. Both the day-to-day role and the Strike Force work are important and must be treated with a high level of urgency. One can't suffer in favor of the other.
- » Choose to inspire them as you describe why you selected them for the Strike Force based on their ability to do great things with you on The Culture Project while also doing their "day job."
- » Tell them about the two meetings per week to start the initiative as well as what you'll be working on right out of the gate.

Now that you have the general construct of the Strike Force defined, it's time to identify specifically who will be joining you on this journey.

Warning: This is a pivotal juncture. You are assembling a group that is going to help you reset the organization. It's entirely too easy (and damaging) to fall into the trap of stacking the Strike Force with those leaders that you met with on Day 6. This will sandbag your efforts and water down the results as you accommodate the legacy culture. While it might be that you can identify one or two members of your leadership team that have been in your ear for just this sort of reset, be very careful and trust your gut implicitly by holding the bar high. In the days ahead, I'll be offering some great ideas on how to think about surrounding yourself with a Strike Force that's built to rock The Culture Project.

DAY 9: NAME YOUR "RISING STAR"

A candidate to strongly consider for your Strike Force is the "Rising Star." Scan the landscape for young, dynamic thinkers that you'd like to mentor. It doesn't matter how young or inexperienced they might be. In fact, that can be extremely effective and useful as they represent the team members that are just starting to rise through the ranks. They will exhibit certain qualities and attributes that will be extremely valuable to consider.

Their expectations, opinions, and inclination to incorporate technology into most everything will offer perspective that would otherwise come via the regurgitation of research from the mouths of more experienced people that really don't represent these characteristics.

TODAY

Think through the below areas and attributes as you create a short list of Rising Star candidates to consider for your Strike Force:
- » They've been with your organization for at least two years.
- » They are either in the technology group or work with a team or department that leverages key technology tools and applications.
- » This person has been a part of initiatives that you feel have been meaningful and satisfying for the business.
- » Their role to date has included some level of optics or collaboration across multiple teams and departments.
- » You have personally noticed their intelligence and people skills.
- » Your gut tells you that they are professional, curious, and willing to work hard.

DAY 10: IDENTIFY YOUR "MUTED LIEUTENANT"

And how do we identify a Strike Force candidate with more experience? One powerful option is the "Muted Lieutenant." Is there an up-and-comer working for a traditional leader that's been trying to find their voice for change with a forward-thinking mentality? Very often there is someone like this whose voice is being filtered to be more in line with the approach of the more senior executive that they work for.

Not only might this be an amazing opportunity to fill a spot on your Strike Force, it might also give you the opportunity to identify and retain a key leader for the future who might otherwise depart in frustration. And while this might require a delicate touch, it could also have a huge impact on the business (as well as an immensely positive impact on a career).

TODAY

Think through the below areas and attributes as you create a short list of Muted Lieutenant candidates to consider for your Strike Force:

- » They have experience with at least one other organization before joining your firm.
- » They've been with your organization for three to five years; that is, long enough to understand the landscape but not so long as to have become part of the status quo.
- » They work for a leader who tends to have success and always takes the credit themselves.
- » They have been promoted into important roles that support a legacy leader.
- » There's a proven track record of successful initiatives reliant upon technology.
- » Your gut tells you they have untapped leadership qualities.
- » They are articulate and respectful.

DAY 11: HIRE AN "OUTSIDER" FOR YOUR STRIKE FORCE

Whenever someone is focused and spending time and energy building or maintaining something important, their perspective is completely enveloped by these activities and the associated outcomes. Attitudes, perspectives, processes, roles, and the like are the forces behind this current. And before long it's carrying you, your outlook, and your approach.

It's just like when you go into the ocean for a swim. Many times, as you relax among the waves, the current will move you down the beach. It just happens. The same dynamic is true at work. So, the trick is how, as a leader, do you keep yourself in check? How do you not get swept along by the current of your existing modus operandi? You need to break free and establish new factors that create a bigger and better current. To do that, you need perspective outside and free of your everyday reality.

Bringing in an "Outsider," a consultant, to be your confidant is significant. That being said, you must guard and protect this confidant from getting caught in your existing current. Don't keep this person and their team on site too long, too often. You must avoid the trap that most businesses fall into by stationing these assets on site, giving them a desk, a computer, a company email address, etc. Think of your business as a bubble. Keep your "Reality Checker" outside of the bubble. Let them come in and not become brainwashed with the way things are. Let them go through discovery, understand how things work, and then be open to their observations.

When you seek and engage this confidant (individual or organization), you need to be certain that you're going to get a taste of reality from them. They are going to tell you the unfiltered truth (with respect, of course) They are going to help you see the waste, infighting, and politics that's occurring right under your nose. They are going to call you out a bit on what they know you are tolerating or blind to within your organization. If this person or group is worth their weight, you're going to be disappointed in yourself. You've prided yourself on being a great leader, someone who has always abhorred mediocrity. And your Reality Checker is going to give it to you straight.

Outsiders have heard it all before.

DAY 11: HIRE AN "OUTSIDER" FOR YOUR STRIKE FORCE

- » They know when you have someone on your leadership team that's not pulling their weight.
- » They know about those in Sales who are not hitting their numbers.
- » They know when your technology group is stuck and not looking into innovative tools and platforms for you to improve the business and its overall productivity.

Can all of this be hiding in plain sight? Yes, it can. And it does. It might not be these exact examples, but you have some version of nonsense and you need this outside perspective to help you identify it. Then you can build what will become a self-evident business case that provides the impetus to change it all. And the Outsider plays a key role as someone that holds you accountable.

Not only are these confidants useful in identifying the broken attributes of your business culture, but they are also great at maintaining perspective and guiding you with sound advice. Staying outside the bubble helps your Reality Checker disrupt your tendencies to protect those that you've been shielding for years by allowing subpar work and the spending of money on initiatives that, deep down, you know are poorly managed.

These resources are a legitimate requirement and typically worth every cent that you pay them. Without them, you'll have people who have been wearing the rose-colored glasses that only match the past. It's time for fresh eyes, ears, and ideas.

TODAY

Think through the following attributes as you create a short list of Outsider candidates that you might know. Also consider calling other leaders in your industry to ask for potential candidates that aren't currently in your network of contacts.

- » You must find someone that has a wide understanding of technology.
- » Your Outsider must be believable, confident, and respectful.
- » Look for someone that has perspective that illustrates a good blend of looking far down the road as well as a practical understanding of day-to-day business.
- » Find someone who is an entrepreneur and will push you to take action.
- » Meet with your Outsider away from the office whenever possible.
- » While the Outsider can be specific to a role on the Strike Force, many leaders taking on The Culture Project can benefit from leveraging this vital resource from Day 1 as their partner throughout the entire journey.

DAY 12: CHOOSE YOUR "ADMINISTRATOR"

A vital role on your Strike Force is the "Administrator," whose primary responsibility is to diligently keep all of your Strike Force–related meetings and interviews at a cadence that allows for progress and gets everyone what they need so that the team shows up prepared. As well, the Administrator keeps you on target for what you want from team members. If no one owns this role, your efforts can get sidetracked by the day-to-day role and responsibilities from each member of the Strike Force.

The best candidate for the Administrator is the executive assistant (EA) to the leader. This keeps the accountability more centralized to the leader and removes an added layer to the scheduling of meetings and activities, as the EA is positioned to work directly through the leader's availability and schedule in general. That being said, having a strong and consistent Administrator is very important to The Culture Project, and if the EA is not the best fit, defer to a better candidate.

TODAY

Think through the below areas and attributes as you create a short list of Administrator candidates to consider for your Strike Force. The Administrator must have the ability to treat all of the activities as "living and breathing" tasks. Meaning, the efforts are ongoing and have to be closely monitored and require proper attention to stay on course throughout The Culture Project. The Administrator will spend time:

» Setting up a vehicle for group collaboration and communication that includes document sharing, chat groups, audio and video conferencing, etc.
» Maintaining energy and momentum through persistent scheduling, coordination, communication, and progress especially for the inevitable curveballs that will occur
» Prompting you and others daily for deliverables such as required feedback and status
» Communicating with others throughout the organization to schedule required meetings and track down needed information on behalf of the Strike Force
» Supporting the creation of presentations and summaries.

DAY 13: MEET WITH EMPLOYEES FOR A BOTTOM-UP PERSPECTIVE

You and the Strike Force need to talk to the people in the trenches. The folks coming to work each and every day. The talent. And you need to understand how these people are using technology to perform their respective roles and responsibilities. It's not about giving them access to technology but rather integrating how they work with technology to give them access to other people, data, knowledge, collaboration, and innovation.

This concept is more than a nuanced thought. It changes how everyone within the business can think and perform better than ever before. This is how we are going to understand where the mediocrity festers and holds us back from the landscape that we now have to not only be a part of, but also excel within. This is from where change will emanate. Scratch that. *Change* isn't the right word. We need a reset of the organization that is in lockstep with the big-picture goals that you are now focused upon.

TODAY

Meet and engage with groups of employees from various departments and teams. Find out what it's like to leverage the tools that the business has invested in to communicate, collaborate, and be productive. How do people share data and ideas in meetings? How do they get heads-down work done at their desk? How do they receive information from the business? How do they receive support or training? What's it like to start a new job at the company? Using the synthesis of talent and technology as the vehicle to communicate with your people will tell you all you need to know about where you need to urgently address the very core of complacency and legacy thinking at your firm.

Some big questions to get to:

» Is IT thinking of tools that work for themselves or tools that work for the end users throughout the business?

» Is Marketing leveraging technology to support Sales? And is Sales using tech in a way that is aligned with the buyer's needs and preferences?

» Is Finance positioned to understand why people seek to make investments or are they making decisions based solely on the numbers without thought for hidden value in varying forms of ROI?

» Are employees and managers too quick to interpret leadership's words and actions as not wanting to spend money or make changes? If so, how much of the decision-making throughout the firm is based solely on cutting costs rather than more strategic solutions that drive improvements?

These questions and many more will emerge from these meetings. Get ready to hear about the plethora of stupid shit that's gumming up the gears of the business you run: conference rooms reserved but not used thus limiting access to valuable collaboration spaces, amazing sales presentations created but not accessible requiring duplicate efforts to re-create a similar or replica presentation, or perhaps users unable to leverage internal collaboration tools so that they push sensitive client data to their personal email accounts for a frictionless mode of collaborating or working from home. These are just a few examples of what you may find. Don't hide from it; rather use it to fuel your inner fire.

DAY 14: X-RAY FOR FRACTURES BETWEEN HR AND IT

There's talent. And there's technology. Respectively. I say respectively because the traditional silos isolate the ownership, optics, and daily management of each. HR is the de facto lead around people and culture. And of course, the IT department owns the technology infrastructure and solutions that the firm invests in to make services available and reliable. But how do we look at HR and IT together as one force?

When the discrete owners of each silo approach their work, the emphasis is giving people access *to* the technology tools rather than emphasizing productivity *with* the technology tools. There just isn't a focus on making people across the organization more efficient and productive via the workplace technology. What has been a traditional operational model for the sake of efficiency has become a significant hurdle for organizations to attain a higher level of productivity and ROI.

Think about it. At your firm, you will approve projects and rollouts; traditional best practices require that technical experts hand the ball off to project management experts. This highlights within IT the need to meet technical specifications and project milestones. This is an entirely different set of outcomes than having an emphasis on technology *and* people so that they are enabled to use the technology for access to colleagues fueling collaboration as well as access to data and knowledge for individual productivity. This means that it is no longer acceptable for IT and HR to be seen as service centers to the business strictly for their respective domains. They must be strategic partners with the organization and its key stakeholders and must jointly look for opportunities to identify shared goals and outcomes.

Here's a key example of a joint effort by IT and HR that I've successfully set in motion for a number of clients. A Digital Adoption Platform (DAP) can be a key component to the training and enablement efforts as a prescriptive curriculum for the needs of each department, team, or role. And you can create transparency around the process so that employees are challenged to consume the content in a timely fashion along with the rest of their peers. These DAPs can focus on training and upskilling of just about any application or set of tools—Microsoft productivity tools, SAP, Salesforce, etc.—and can be integrated with the Learning

Management System that HR uses for various areas of corporate training. Think of how powerful it can be to give end users a "single pane of glass" to the training and learning content with transparent accountability built in.

TODAY

On this Day 14, the Strike Force's objective is to meet independently with the leadership of each silo and understand exactly where the disconnects are and where there are opportunities to create a higher standard of how your talent and technology keep in lockstep.

Here are some tips on specific elements to focus on during these sessions with IT and HR.

» What is the onboarding process for new hires? Is technology training an important aspect?
» Is it just technical training or are we incorporating business goals with the need to know how to use these tools?
» How well does IT handle training and communicating in general? Stereotypically, technical people aren't always the best at thinking through the user perspective when explaining how to use these tools. Consider that HR, in many ways, are much more expert at training and communicating to people.
» Where are the opportunities for joint efforts to fuse together talent and technology?
» Check out your business on Glassdoor. More and more current and former employees are including technology when critiquing the organization. Even if there isn't a direct technology statement, there might be words describing the organization that are just poison to the future of retaining and attracting talent. Words such as *outdated*, *stodgy*, *cheap*, and

uninformed (as well as many others) are either rooted in technology issues and/or leadership's lack of emphasis on making the business a place without friction. This tells you just how important technology has become for organizations and the act of doing business.

DAY 15: MEET WITH KEY MANAGERS TO ID FRICTION

Friction is everywhere. People in your company feel it during the course of countless interactions. When the gears just don't turn as smoothly as they could or, maybe better put, should. Every time there's interaction between two or more people, between people and data, or even getting one data set to interact with another data set, employees are left to work harder, revisit aspects of the interaction repeatedly, or exercise manual labor. And whenever this happens, people know that it doesn't have to be this difficult.

They are continuously comparing their experiences at work with how they do things in their personal lives. And when it's not as frictionless as their personal technology experiences, the thinking turns into negative critique of the business, festers, and then seeps through the entire organization: The firm is cheap, leadership doesn't care about people or work-life balance, the business doesn't support new ideas, and so on. None of it is conducive to a positive and productive environment.

Before getting started on today's actions, I'd like to introduce a very important concept for you to leverage throughout The Culture Project. I call it the "Three Perspectives Rule" and it's all about context. And when considering context, one size does not fit all. This was something that resonated deeply for me after reading *The Three Laws of Performance* by Steve Zaffron and Dave Logan. The book's authors describe their first law as follows: "How people perform correlates to how situations occur to them." Zaffron and Logan go on to say:

> "Each person assumes that the way things occur for him or her is how they are occurring for another. But situations occur differently for each person. Not realizing this can make another's actions seem out of place."

This is valuable input for the Strike Force's discussions with the key line-of-business managers. Not only can we compare their perspectives to those in IT delivering them the tools to be productive, but we can also compare the perspectives of other related groups or teams that leverage the same technologies as part of an interdependent business process.

Take for example the interactions between Marketing and Sales. You, of course, want your sales team to be successful.

Sales obviously relies on other groups such as Marketing and Technology: Marketing from the standpoint of having access to the quality content and collateral to be used as tools throughout the sales process; Technology comes into play because tools and platforms are needed to effectively interact with both the content and collateral as well as the marketing department and the potential buyers themselves. How does all of this integrate into a frictionless process that considers the goals and perspectives of the three constituencies—the marketer, the seller, and the buyer?

Applying this rule across all business groups is quite powerful. By applying the "Three Perspectives Rule," you're challenged to identify and examine vital interactions and how they "occur" to each related individual, team, or department that have their own realities, incentives ,and perceptions to consider.

TODAY

Meet with key managers of business groups or teams. You have two overarching goals as you and the Strike Force engage these important people. First, look to discover their perspective on technology and how it helps their team be productive. Second, identify where IT and HR need to better collaborate around shared goals and outcomes to help align context between intersecting groups and initiatives.

Here are specific directions to meet these two overarching goals for today:

- » Understand an overview of business processes that particular groups use to deliver on their commitments.
- » What other groups within the firm do they rely on for data and knowledge?
- » How do these groups communicate and collaborate?
- » Where and how does technology impact these interactions? Are they positive?
- » Does the IT team understand the importance as well as the mechanics of these interactions?
- » What ideas does each respective key manager have for improving these interactions?
- » What root issues have prevented them from being more productive and efficient?

This is a wonderful opportunity to uncover and understand misaligned talent and technology and the profoundly negative impact it's having throughout your organization. This friction exists in many other areas of the business. Finance, Procurement, Operations, Customer Service, Account Management, and every other department are all ripe for this friction. All groups rely on interactions with other people, teams, information, and knowledge. And there are multiple angles to fixing it.

Go identify it all. Then set your mind on fixing it.

PHASE II: ACTIVATE

DAY 16: REVIEW THE GAPS BETWEEN TALENT AND TECH

You've built your Strike Force with intelligent, innovative, and aggressive colleagues from different areas of the firm. There have been some really productive days collecting information from various corners of the organization. It's vital that you and the Strike Force review the gaps identified between what the end users experience, what IT and HR see as drivers to deliver around, and, of course, your leadership team's view of the firm and its future.

Just as in the model of sales alignment when we applied the Three Perspectives Rule on Day 15 (e.g., efforts to understand the friction between the marketer, the seller, and the buyer), it is essential for the Strike Force to understand where gaps and friction exist between these three perspectives—leadership, HR/IT, and employees. This is at the very core of what you will attack and reconcile in your business. In fact, it's literally the vehicle you are using to drive The Culture Project.

This is the perfect time to mentor your Strike Force through further understanding and applying the Three Perspectives Rule to identify friction and fractures in your discussions to date. Empowering them to understand and apply this rule in the coming days and weeks will result in serious momentum. The Strike Force and you will be energized as you view The Culture Project through the same lens to understand today's reality versus how those unique perspectives should be aligned. I strongly recommend that you preach Growth Mindset (from Carol Dweck's book *Mindset*) and acknowledge that seeking perfection is the enemy of getting good things done.

Be aware that you can overwhelm the team if you get too detailed in your work together thus far. Leave that for the days to come. Continue to align your Strike Force with your mandate to yourself and your staunch unwillingness to negotiate with complacency and mediocrity. Review and discuss to generate the appropriate update you will provide to the senior leadership on Day 17. Along with energizing those around you (both your Strike Force and your leadership team), you'll feel a renewed commitment to be a genuine and strong leader. You'll be emboldened as your message motivates and inspires your team and, over time, your entire organization.

TODAY

Build a presentation with the Strike Force that will, in essence, be the Strike Force providing you and the leadership team with an update of the activities to date as well as some top-level findings, which review the overarching issues discovered while talking to the various constituencies on Days 13, 14, and 15. The Strike Force will quickly understand their mission to update the leadership team while not becoming overtly confrontational and coming across as throwing anyone under the bus at such an early stage. The presentation that you create today should not directly challenge any leadership team member's role or responsibilities. Here's what I recommend for you and the Strike Force as you structure the presentation.

» Create a slide for each respective day that gives an overview of what you and the Strike Force did on Day 13 (bottom-up discovery with employees), Day 14 (X-ray for fractures by meeting with HR and IT), and Day 15 (detecting friction by meeting with key line-of-business managers).

» Each of these overview slides should inform the leadership team of who you met with and the kind of questions you were asking.

» For each day's overview slide, prepare an accompanying slide with high level examples of interesting information that was shared.

» When preparing for the presentation, you and the Strike Force must keep in mind that you are not trying to get any specific points across. The purpose is to keep the leadership team in the loop and give them this touch-point to hear high level information that

> allows them to feel safe and begin making the shift to align their thinking with The Culture Project.
>
> » During preparation, I would also suggest that you help orchestrate the Strike Force to do most or all of the talking rather than open up to Q and A that is likely to pull the conversation into more specific areas that will precipitate unwanted confrontation or resentment.

Warning: This Day 17 meeting being set up as the Strike Force updating you and your leadership team should not be interpreted as you fire-walling yourself from the activities and findings. In fact, you should be willing to acknowledge and confirm findings throughout the presentation to illustrate that you support what's being done. More on that in Day 17.

DAY 17: THE STRIKE FORCE UPDATES YOUR LEADERSHIP TEAM

You've set the tone with your Strike Force. Over the coming days, you'll continue by busting down the legacy guardrails and brainstorming around "what ifs" and "blue sky" concepts and ideas. You will start to feel a sense of optimism and excitement about what you can accomplish together.

There will be a sense of "Why didn't we do this sooner?" As the leader, you will become acutely aware of the legacy-driven conversations and limited perspectives that you've allowed or even fostered in the past. Today, however, you are in a much different place. You're starting to play again. You'll be energized to transform your culture from a passive maze of suboptimal (but yet somehow acceptable) policies and behaviors into one that is ripe for fresh thinking, new ideas, productivity, and value. You are disrupting your culture and only good things will come of it.

Ironically, you'll also need to address the reality of being uncomfortable. In fact, we are at a crucial crossroads whereas many leaders lose steam and begin to negotiate with legacy factors thus lowering the bar on future aspirations (consciously or sub-consciously). What are those factors? They are the legacy leaders, their processes, perspectives, and goals that are aligned with everything that you are looking to break or evolve as part of The Culture Project.

So, what's the answer? It's vital to restate the obvious. If you want The Culture Project to be successful, there is no way to avoid the root problems of your business' current state. Recall Day 4 and the acknowledgement that this was going to be difficult. You are promoting change and that is uncomfortable especially for senior leaders. Again, this is unavoidable, and you must stay resolute.

TODAY

Hold a meeting for the Strike Force to present to your senior leadership team. This update offers you a wonderful opportunity to position The Culture Project as a significant benefit for your leadership team. It also offers the leadership team the opportunity to see and understand that these Strike Force members, under your guidance, are here to offer everyone new energy and ideas.

We are still in a very early and delicate stage. You and the Strike Force prepared a presentation on Day 16 that would not be confrontational but rather provide a high-level overview of what you have experienced thus far. The purpose of this meeting is to bring along your leadership, not taking them on in a "moment of truth" that will risk even the best chief executives and Strike Force getting neutered by the leadership team. Allow your fellow leaders to begin the process of truly understanding to what you are committing the business (and them).

I've seen varying reactions in meetings such as this. And these reactions will often telegraph how your leadership team will digest and process The Culture Project moving forward. Some leaders choose to be quiet and just listen. Others ask many questions. Others might subtly, or not so subtly, attempt to contrast their experience with those of Strike Force members. The defensiveness may very well begin to show itself, however, there's no need to react today. Allow your leaders the time and space to truly understand your genuine motives. Here's my recommendation on shaping this agenda:

» General introductions
» An opening statement from you, the leader, about why The Culture Project is so important

> » Designated members of the Strike Force should run through the presentation created on Day 16 highlighting the work to date along with some very high-level observations.
> » A preview of the Strike Force's activities in the days ahead
> » Avoid questions and answers between your leadership team and the Strike Force so that you minimize the opportunity for a quagmire of legacy-driven conversation and/or confrontation

One method that has worked well for me in the past is to give the Strike Force 30 to 45 minutes for the introduction and presentation while leaving time within the scheduled meeting time for you to discuss a specific unrelated but simple issue with the leadership team after dismissing the Strike Force. Once the Strike Force has been dismissed, quickly work through that simple issue then ask the leadership team what they thought of the Strike Force's presentation. This will give you an opportunity to understand each leader's perspective in a group setting without a "moment of truth" while the Strike Force is present.

During the presentation and after the Strike Force has left the meeting, take note of body language or anything else that gives insight as to whom on your leadership team might be ripe to join the Strike Force efforts over the coming days (especially as you'll begin to initiate exercises that brainstorm around the information collected thus far). While it can be devastating to bring negativity into these upcoming efforts, it can also be extremely valuable to add leaders if, and only if, they "get it." If you are on the fence with anyone, they aren't the right fit for joining the Strike Force's efforts. Be careful and trust your gut in bringing individuals into the fold *only* when you know that they are ready.

DAY 17: THE STRIKE FORCE UPDATES YOUR LEADERSHIP TEAM

If this presentation is done well, the leadership team, the Strike Force, and you get a jolt and the longstanding departmental silos continue to be put on notice. This doesn't mean that the legacy perspective has been squeezed out of everyone that's been enabling mediocrity. You're going to find that once you see what's happening in your company, the importance of this work will be obvious. What you'll also see is how deep this legacy perspective is and how hard it is for some people to let it go. This meeting continues to provide you with the optics required to win over senior leaders as you look ahead to Day 22, when you'll be taking inventory of those that are supporting The Culture Project as well as those that need more convincing.

DAY 18: ATTACK THE LOW-HANGING FRUIT

You and the Strike Force have summarized the gaps and reviewed as a team. You've focused the collective lens on the types of friction and fractures that you want to rid from the organization.

Now is the time to get more specific with your Strike Force as you prepare to take action. Keep in mind, responding to friction doesn't necessarily require spending a ton of money. As well, recall what I mentioned in Day 16; it's more about taking action than it's about getting things perfect (Growth Mindset!).

TODAY

Create a "hit list" of initiatives that will be your initial ideas for laser-focused actions letting everyone know you mean business. These initiatives should certainly address any legitimate risks that have come to light (security, compliance, etc.) as you begin to solve for some of the real issues and breakdowns that you've uncovered thus far. Your Strike Force will contribute ideas that they are passionate about. Take the options and vet them as a team. Some might be the initial steps or first phase of longer initiatives. Others might be nagging technology issues that no one has dealt with. Or it could be something fresh and new that represents what people should expect more of. When you activate this project in the days ahead, this hit list is the equivalent of a first impression. You know that you get only one chance at a first impression. Make it count!

As you put together this very important hit list, consider the following options or scenarios for guidance:

- » Something that impacts as many people as possible.
- » Anything remotely relevant that is considered by many to be long overdue
- » Something that can be quick and easy that helps create momentum
- » Anything that makes you more secure *and* helps productivity (yes this exists!!)
- » Something that has surfaced before but made you uncomfortable or even scared
- » Something that opens that door a bit more for the inspiration required to really get your leadership team and the business aligned and back on the road to stellar outcomes.

DAY 19: CHALLENGE CURRENT PRACTICES

One of the main drivers to considering candidates for your Strike Force was finding diversity of thought from people within your organization. It would be too easy to label this as "outside the box" thinking. It's more than that. This is about shedding all of the preset assumptions that become fixed over time as you work day-in and day-out within the same organization, with the same people pursuing the same goals and objectives as laid out by the same leadership team.

Here are just some examples of the presets that likely exist within your organization in one form or another: They'll never pay for that, they will never approve that change, he or she doesn't believe in that, people will never use it here, the culture here is different. You get the idea. Why do these preset assumptions even exist?

Over time leadership becomes wary of the motives and strategies of those throughout the organization who manage the budgeting and planning for the respective lines of business or departments that oversee internal functions such as IT, HR, facilities, and finance. These leaders and managers throughout the organization are heavily influenced by their own interpretation of senior leadership's words and deeds. As the constituencies continue to work together, muscle memory sets in and—if not disrupted—allows mediocrity and complacency to become this invisible force that negatively impacts day-to-day thinking as well as longer-term and innovative thinking.

What you need to do is rely more on your Strike Force. You sat with these employees and talked to them about their roles and how technology produces friction. You certainly would have heard things that make you scratch your head or wonder how people came to do things the way they are being done. This bottom-up view provided terrific leads into where exactly legacy thinking is slowing down productivity.

TODAY

Assign different Strike Force members to the areas of the business that your gut tells you are being impacted by compartmentalized, stale thinking. When you send them out, ask them to come back to you with three perspectives of the same process. As in Days 15 and 16, here the Three Perspectives Rule is not three people with the same function, but rather three groups or roles that are affected by the same process. This will tell you if and how each group or team is applying legacy presets to their part in the process and ultimately contributing to lackluster results.

Here are a few examples of where you can send your Strike Force:

» **The sales process:** Where is sales collateral produced (marketer), how is it accessed and used (seller), and how is it communicated to the potential client (buyer). The three perspectives here are the marketer, the seller, and the buyer. Are all efforts throughout the sales process aligned?

» **The procurement process:** What are the rules of engagement for the organization to purchase products/services (finance), what is the process to identify service providers and solicit proposals (procurement), and, of course, what is the experience of using those products and services within the organization once they are purchased (business users)? The three perspectives here are the finance group, procurement, and the business user.

» **Onboarding:** When new people are hired, how are they communicated with before their first day at your organization and during the first weeks of their employment (HR), how do they come to understand both the technology that the firm uses as well as the tools and apps specific to their role (IT), and how do they understand how to apply all of this information to be productive as soon as possible (line-of-business manager). The three perspectives here are HR, IT, and the group manager responsible for the new employee.

Note: If you invited someone from your leadership team to join you for this meeting with the Strike Force, connect with them afterward one-on-one to get their impression of what they heard. Are they truly on board? Are they excited to be a part of these conversations? Do they have any thoughts about others on the leadership team that can be more involved with the right attitude and perspective?

DAY 20: EXPLORE THE BOUNDARIES OF THE FUTURE

While attacking the legacy thinking as we did in Day 19, it's imperative to inspire new thinking around the everyday ways of working. It's also utterly essential and foundational for innovation and the future of your business. It's completely dysfunctional for an organization rife with friction between people and knowledge (data!) to expect new and creative ideas be effective in helping grow and evolve the bigger picture.

Again, as in Day 19, this will start with your Strike Force and then emanate through the organization over time. You need to be the facilitator of a session that challenges each and every member of your Strike Force to remove the barriers that continuously put guardrails on the ideation process.

In this session, your role is to let your team do the thinking. Delegate brainstorming to them so that you can keep focused on making sure that there aren't any limiting forces that enter the equation. Make sure that, for the purposes of this exercise, the Strike Force knows there's no budget, no restraints for people to learn, no managers that can get in the way, no barriers to new technologies, or anything else that can prevent people from thinking broadly and deeply. Today is solely about ideas that might change the perspective or approach to, not only how people work internal to your organization, but also how your team thinks about, creates, and delivers your products and services.

Day 20 is one of my favorite days. It is absolutely exhilarating to be a valued member of the Strike Force and to be liberated from constraints, both real and imagined, to think freely and openly about the possibilities. It can be even more enjoyable and eye-opening for you, as the facilitator, to mentor this group through such conversations. As you hear your team start to hit their stride in this session, you will feel a sense of elation. You will be energized and inspired by your people. And rather than focus on the past by getting down on yourself for not engaging people sooner, you should look forward and enjoy being back in the true state of mind of a leader. Enjoy the process of coaching and leading others.

TODAY

Engage in specific conversations and activities that will get your team to explore the boundaries of the future of your organization. Here are my recommendations for driving these conversations and activities.

» Identify technology manufacturers specific to your industry. You and the Strike Force should schedule team visits to their showrooms and get their pitch and perspective on where the industry is going. While their "blue sky" pitch will be tilted to their own solutions, it can be very enlightening to see how they are thinking about the future.

» Engage with your reps from vendors like both Microsoft and Amazon for their respective pitch and perspective. What are they doing with other firms in your vertical now? How are they thinking about your future and things such as the cloud, analytics, and machine learning?

» Engage other partners or even competitors in your industry. Are there new ways of working together? What challenges are they having and how are they thinking about solving them?

» Discuss the possibility of developing a summer internship program in partnership with a top university.

» Have these young, tech savvy minds focus on a NextGen project for six to eight weeks that's all about the future of your industry and how your firm can evolve accordingly.

Note: It may be difficult for you to facilitate this work alone. Handing the reins over to the Outsider to facilitate some or all of this conversation is a great option. And always remember that the Outsider is well positioned to identify and call out any limited thinking due to legacy perception or bias.

This Day 20 meeting is about forming a list of ideas such as the ones listed above. Keep pushing your team to think differently and be open-minded to meeting and talking with people that might at first seem disconnected to their roles and/or your organization's history.

PHASE III: CONVERT

DAY 21: DOCUMENT YOUR PLANS FOR ESTABLISHING "ACCESS"

Over the past eight days of The Culture Project, you and the Strike Force have been extremely productive talking to various constituencies in the business: end users, line-of-business managers, IT, HR, the executive leadership team, and so on.

The last few of those days were spent brainstorming around all of the information that was collected, absorbed, and understood to drive discussions and activities to generate ideas and options to pursue. You did this as part of your efforts to establish ideas for quick wins, attacking legacy bias as well as understanding the "blue sky" options before you.

The challenge now is to take these ideas and options and begin to define how you'll move forward with tangible plans to pursue the best options for your organization.

The question becomes: "How do we organize and formulate our plan for moving forward?." The answer is "Access." Access will be how you drive this initiative forward. And it is all about allowing people and information to Access colleagues and information in a seamless, secure, and compliant manner. Most, if not all, of your employees should be considered a "knowledge worker" which is defined by the *New Oxford American Dictionary* as, "a person whose job involves handling or using information." The initiatives you formulate must be anchored by the quest to create access within your organization. Recasting your culture around the alignment of talent and technology means creating this access without friction so that people and information can interact removing barriers to higher levels of productivity.

TODAY

The rubber hits the road starting now. You and your Strike Force will take all of the options and ideas that came out of Days 18, 19, and 20 and commit to initiatives that will bring Access to your organization. And though the best ideas to create the highest levels of Access should be front and center, realities such as budget and timing are also extremely important. Here are my recommendations on formulating a plan by creating three lists that will recast your culture.

» **List 1:** Establish a list of five initiatives from your Day 18 hit list that you will implement as Quick Wins. As a reminder, these Quick Wins must impact as many people as possible, be visible to all, bring positive momentum, and open the door a bit more for the inspiration required to really get your leadership and the business aligned and back on the road to stellar outcomes. *Reminder:* A Quick Win can't be so small and trivial that it doesn't match a real commitment to change. You must look long and hard at the opportunities for initial success points. These opportunities must exhibit characteristics that give leaders credibility quickly to build immediate trust.

» **List 2:** Establish a list of six to eight initiatives that emanate from Strike Force efforts on Day 19 to identify legacy practices that need to be attacked. You'll recall sending the Strike Force out to specific business areas and leveraging the Three Perspectives Rule to understand what exactly was holding back key areas of information flow and collaboration within certain teams or departments. This list should

focus on the ones that will be the most important and influential to both productivity and user engagement.
- » **List 3:** Establish a list of two to three forward-thinking initiatives. On Day 20, you facilitated a meeting that encouraged the Strike Force to shed any limitations in creating ideas that will inform the future of the business. This list is important in that you need to help the Strike Force distill these options into a short list worthy of pursuit. Keeping this list short allows you and your team to follow the breadcrumbs toward tangible projects that will change the future of your organization.
- » Throughout your discussions with the Strike Force, your leadership team, and all employees (including managers and departmental leaders), the ideas have flowed freely as you worked hard to minimize any limiting factors. To illustrate to your team that no idea is a bad idea, you should maintain a "parking lot" for ideas that fail to make the final cut. Though these ideas did not make it to one of these three lists, they can and should be referred to in the future as new options to help remind you and your team of the process that you went through.

DAY 22: SUPERHEROES AND SATYA NADELLA

Years ago, I read a book by Amy Cuddy, *Presence*, which focuses on confidence—particularly the means and ways of getting into a positive mindset.

One of the techniques Cuddy reveals comes to mind when I think of preparing to be a catalyst for the change that The Culture Project demands. Utilizing "Power Posing," you stand in front of a mirror and take the posture of a superhero. Chest out, hands at your side, chin up, and one foot ahead of the other. The science behind this move is that physiologically, your facial expression and posture, can impact your state of mind: You feel strong, confident—even invincible. I love this concept when it comes to becoming a catalyst for The Culture Project. Because you must think, act, and follow through like a "super leader" armed with resolve.

Without this, the organization and the people that work for it will suffer over time. To avoid this, you'll need to lead the leaders and employees mentioned in Day 4: those who are kicking and screaming through the uncomfortable process of change. Remember, *you* are the one that recognized the need for The Culture Project. It was you that initiated and followed through yourself over the past 21 days rather than delegating to the traditional silos.

Many leaders have a great way of keeping themselves accountable. Sometimes it can be as simple as telling a spouse or confidant what they are going to do because once they "say it out loud," it triggers that drive and fear of failure within themselves. In other cases, we rely on the plan we develop and those that we identify as its supporters. They help bring the plan through development and keep us accountable for following through.

My favorite example of a leader's unwavering approach to changing their organization is Microsoft's Satya Nadella. When he started his tenure as CEO, Microsoft was sliding more and more toward irrelevancy as the company continued to focus on the most profitable aspect of their business: selling software licenses to corporations that they've held captive as clients for decades. Meanwhile, companies such as Apple, Amazon, Salesforce, and others had become the darlings of Wall Street, businesses, and consumers as they developed cutting-edge technology and leveraged "the cloud." Microsoft had its seminal moment, shifting to innovative offerings that were the next generation of their own corporate products (among others for consumers, such as Xbox). But this wasn't an easy transition by any stretch of the imagination.

Nadella had to convince his entire organization (including the CFO) that Microsoft must forego the more profitable software licensing that had gotten the company to the top of the business universe in order to sell subscriptions to their cloud solutions in Office 365 (now Microsoft 365) and Azure. Think of that conversation with the CFO:

> "Yes, I understand we have these corporate clients captive, and it's a hugely profitable endeavor to be charging for software license renewals and upgrades, but, in the future, this model won't exist. So, let's incentivize our sales force to sell our new, less profitable cloud products and begin to phase out the legacy software license business."

I can see it now—mouths open aghast and you could have heard a pin drop.

OK, perhaps it was more of a process than a singular conversation, but just imagine the pushback throughout many areas of the business. Every single nook and cranny of Microsoft's business and culture was focused on developing, selling, upgrading, and marketing software licenses. Can you fathom a bigger challenge to employees' approach to their jobs, their roles, their habits, and their sense of security? And it wasn't only the employees at-large. It was C-Level leaders, managers, probably even members of the board.

Amy Cuddy's *Presence* didn't come out until 2015, but I'm guessing there were more than a few times that Nadella had to stick out his chest and remind himself that he needed the confidence of Superman to persevere through an onslaught of challenges, pessimism, and even dissent within the very business he was leading.

Microsoft is one of the most famous businesses in history. The very will to lead could have been rinsed right out of Nadella, given the pushback from stakeholders both within as well as beyond the walls of his organization. Although it was daunting, he was unwavering. Microsoft's stock was just below $38 per share the day before Nadella's tenure began in February 2014. At the close of the market on August 28, 2020, the stock was trading around $227 per share. I'll let you be the judge as to whether Nadella was successful in leading his organization through a massive change.

TODAY

Spend time looking for leaders that have either successfully brought massive changes to their respective businesses or are currently in the midst of doing so. They don't necessarily have to mirror the exact challenges that you have decided to confront. These issues can be anything that a leader decided to spearhead in order to flourish or even to survive a future that required a culture directly aligned with new and improved goals and objectives.

Here are a few case studies from the past as well as a couple of current transformational efforts that, along with those that you have researched yourself, can offer you inspiration and motivation for The Culture Project:

- » Jeff Bezos and Amazon's pivot from online bookstore to a cloud behemoth
- » Mary Barra's efforts to position General Motors for an electric and self-driving future
- » Howard Schultz' shifting Starbucks from bureaucracy to customers after the 2008 financial crisis
- » Rose Marie Bravo and Angela Ahrendts leading the outstanding global growth of Burberry
- » Lou Gerstner's turnaround of IBM
- » Indra Nooyi's PepsiCo shift from soda to sustainability-minded food, snack, and beverage company
- » Steve Jobs and his second coming at Apple that resulted in the iPhone.

DAY 23: KNOW WHO IS IN, OUT, AND UNDECIDED

Changing the culture, mindset, and trajectory of a business is much like preparing for, and ultimately winning, an election. You will have those who are for you, those who are against you, and then you'll have those who are undecided. You'll need a strategy for dealing with the leaders and stakeholders who fit within each segment.

For those who support you, you'll want to continue to communicate with them effectively so that they feel and see the progress. Keeping them interested and excited is imperative. Not only do you want to make sure that the naysayers don't chip away at their positive outlook, but you also want to use their positive outlook and enthusiasm to convert the undecided (and hopefully a few naysayers) into supporters.

For those who choose not to support you (malicious compliance!), you will need to figure out how to quarantine this negativity. As you further socialize change among leadership and then, of course, the employee base, those who don't support you will be uncomfortable. Remember, you are challenging their domain, comfort zone, and sense of control over their job and subordinates. In some instances, change might be the right answer for a leader or stakeholder as well as for the organization.

As for the undecided, this is where your enormous opportunity lies to win over people and create momentum that eventually either will bring your nonsupporters into the mix or create a culture and system that rejects that type of negativity. The undecided might be wary because initially when you announce to the firm that change is afoot, they might think to themselves, "I've heard this before." And they likely have. This time, though, you will make it different. This is directly connected to Days 18 and 19 and the work you did identifying opportunities to make immediate change as well as what we'll do on Days 25 and 26 respectively.

TODAY

Get prepared and catalog your supporters, nonsupporters, and those who can go either way. You heard from employees about their reality and the friction they encounter daily. You know where certain leaders and stakeholders contributed to much of this. You spoke to leaders and line-of-business managers directly. You also had the Strike Force present an overview to the leadership team after meeting with various constituencies throughout the firm. Undoubtedly, you heard, saw, or felt some things that raised flags. You need to be honest with yourself as you go through this exercise. You must be mindful of who are your allies and fellow agents for change while also knowing who is likely to be a drag on what you are setting out to accomplish. Being prepared for the various reactions to The Culture Project will allow you to work with your Strike Force appropriately and leverage the supporters, keep the naysayers in check, and convert the undecided to create an unstoppable force that changes the trajectory of your business.

DAY 24: STAY COMMITTED TO YOUR PLAN

You and your Strike Force have done some wonderful work over these last 23 days. You've taken stock of those executives around you, visited the people in the trenches, and connected with those who lead departments that really impact your employees and bottom line. You've also reacquainted yourself with a few notable business turnaround stories that required great, strong leadership.

This is the ideal jumping-off point to affecting the changes that are needed. Start engaging people more than you have been. Begin to make a list of decisions that you know are tough and best for the business—and formulate a plan to tackle them. This won't necessarily result in firing a bunch of your loyal colleagues. Perhaps it's putting them in a different place to succeed. Perhaps you can pull them into your plans and coach them to be a part of the change. It's a poignant time for you to help people succeed in ways that are aligned with the business' needs and best interests, perhaps more so than any other time during your tenure. The ability to communicate with people and allow them to envision their roles and common goals are huge factors in bringing about loyalty and inspiration.

TODAY

Document the top three behaviors that you need to exhibit at this moment. These should be three strong traits that you expect of yourself. By all means, use the compelling business stories that you researched in Day 22 as inspiration. What behaviors were prevalent in the turnaround stories that resonated with you the most? Perhaps more research or training is needed if you think some of these attributes aren't necessarily second nature to you. Here are a few questions that you can ask yourself:

- » Will you remain resolute and tough?
- » Will you be empathetic?
- » Will you commit to leveraging technology more so than you have in the past?
- » How will you keep close to the pulse of the organization rather than over-delegating to others?

You know yourself. Pick these three important behaviors by promoting your strengths and supporting your weaknesses.

DAY 25: PUBLICLY COMMIT TO "THE WHY" OF THE CULTURE PROJECT

Tell your organization "why" the change is coming: Why it will not jeopardize their status. Why it will facilitate their performance. Why it will drive higher levels of productivity and personal fulfillment.

This is a much wiser and enlightened approach than what corporations traditionally are wired to do. It might be more in line with a small business or a startup and its exactly what bigger siloed businesses need to "borrow" from their more-nimble competitors.

In a nutshell, this is the essence of true, inspirational leadership.

Let's put this in perspective. The evolution of corporate structures brought about efficiencies and effectiveness for larger organizations with money and resources to manage. The silos became inevitable and pushed people and organizations into processed thinking.

Quite often, true change cannot reshape an organization until a new leader is recruited or an existing leader is revitalized: one who has the skills and the track record of achievement to illustrate the "why."

As inspirational leadership guides strategically appropriate elements of change, team members will see it and start to believe it. And once they start to believe in the new direction, they will invest in it.

Here's the big payoff: Once we reach that tipping point, we begin to see communication, collaboration, and productivity converge and rise in tandem.

TODAY

Personally present the outline of your plan to the entire organization. While an off-site company meeting isn't necessary, it's not a bad investment. However, if that is too difficult logistically, an all-hands 8 a.m. meeting for 60 to 90 minutes that is streamed across all office locations and conference rooms is the minimum requirement. We want everyone to hear directly from you. This is your opportunity to make a first and lasting impression on the entire organization. Put it in a way that leaves no doubt that you are serious. Then prepare yourself to act and provide them evidence of what's to come. Here is how you should approach this company-wide meeting:

» Your introduction should be about the organization's history and accomplishments.

» Introduce The Culture Project and why you feel it is so important to understand how and why the organization should challenge itself to better align talent and technology.

» Give an overview of the "blue sky" exercise and what the firm will pursue for the future.

» Provide an overview of how everyone needs to challenge themselves to be uncomfortable as we consider the approach to work and outcomes.

» Give the specific plans of how you plan on going about these changes.

» Give them an overview of what to expect tomorrow, Day 26—your finalized list of initiatives that you are going to activate tomorrow.

Note: You might have noticed that throughout this book I refer to the previous day or the following day by its number without using the terms *yesterday* or *tomorrow*. I do that because, as I pointed out in the Introduction, these 30 days aren't necessarily contiguous. However, I can't state this enough: Day 26 *must* happen the very next day (as in tomorrow) after Day 25. You must follow up immediately to engage your plans after making your presentation and announce what you are committing to.

DAY 26: MOVE QUICKLY LIKE AN ENTREPRENEUR TO INSPIRE

Inspiring employees is the most important aspect of The Culture Project as the business blossoms into a functional and modern organization. However, before you can inspire you must garner a higher level of trust.

How do we recapture trust? How do we bring employees back to that feeling that they had on their first day of work? That time when they were curious, excited, and willing to help the business be successful and reap the rewards themselves? Your actions must be ingredients to elicit this willingness. There's nothing more powerful to combat the eye rolls you saw at yesterday's "big change announcement" than quick and meaningful improvement. Offering initiatives that promise legitimate improvement is essential right on the heels of your presentation yesterday.

TODAY

Send out a company-wide email communicating more details about the low-hanging fruit Quick Win initiatives that commence *today*. Yes, this email should come directly from you—not your EA or corporate communications or the head of HR or the CIO. It must come from you. Here's what I recommend when creating this communication.

- » Include all five of the Quick Win initiatives that you finalized on Day 21.
- » For each initiative, be sure to have a good description of what you are doing and why you're pursuing these improvements.
- » State who is the owner of each of these five Quick Win initiatives.
- » Manage expectations by offering a timeframe for each initiative while also committing to updating everyone at a cadence that makes sense (more frequent updates are better).
- » Explain how you will be connected to each initiative throughout the process.

Remember: The initiatives that you are describing today cannot come across as so small and trivial that they appear as though they're not a real commitment to change. You looked long and hard at the opportunities for initial success points. These Quick Win opportunities that you and the Strike Force determined were the best path forward must exhibit characteristics that give leaders credibility quickly to build immediate trust.

Offering these initiatives that promise legitimate improvement is essential right on the heels of your presentation yesterday.

DAY 27: ACTIVELY WIN OVER THE UNDECIDED

It's time to get competitive and win. On Day 23, you did a scan of the leadership team and key stakeholders to better understand who was with you, against you, and then, of course, who could go either way. This is the undecided segment of influencers that I earlier compared to the undecided segment of voters that come into play during an election. And just as in the election process, you need to implement your strategy to address those that are undecided. Now's the time!

You have communicated the "why" to the masses and launched your quick and decisive efforts to deal with the low-hanging fruit Quick Wins. Take out that list you formed on Day 21 and give it a quick read through and see if anything has changed. My guess is that there won't be a significant change. There might be a few key people who have shown their cards, and you've come to the realization that they were more uncomfortable with your new energy and direction than they originally let on. And then there might be a few more that have seen and heard some things that have excited them enough to emerge as supporters. That being said, your undecided list is what needs attention now.

TODAY

Engage key people who you deem to be undecided. Sit with them, ask them what they think, begin to hear their concerns as well as the openings that you see to engage them in a way that makes them feel part of the positive momentum. The time you spend converting some of these employees into supporters is of great use. Don't get frustrated with any that aren't making the transition. Let them continue to experience and see what is taking shape around them. For those who are making progress, see where they can help your mission. Here are some ideas on how to use these new supporters to make serious headway:

» Is there a very influential leader or key stakeholder who could be a break-through? If so, have them meet with your Strike Force and brainstorm around everything that's going on. Be honest and transparent.

» Have a conversation with some of the undecided and analyze their business units or the entire company. Given their skepticism, learn what influences their perspective. Try to understand if the message you've pushed out to the masses resonates. Maybe there is something that doesn't quite connect with a specific business group or type of user. If you discover something new and understandable, perhaps it helps to give others more traction.

» Ask key undecided people to coauthor an approach to their team or department. If you see them start to provide input that is positive, schedule a meeting with their department and let this stakeholder present to the team as well as give you a few minutes to address these users. Illustrate to this leader and their team that you are a true partner.

DAY 28: INSTITUTIONALIZE PERPETUAL LEARNING AND ENABLEMENT

Over the past few days you have communicated to the masses what you are doing, you've strategically launched specific and meaningful initiatives to illustrate that you mean business, and you've actively worked to convert some of the undecided stakeholders to not only support you but also to partner with you and bolster your efforts in a major way.

More succinctly stated: You have made a declaration, you've acted on it, and you've begun to coach your people to join you in reaching your goals for success together.

Going forward this must be an ongoing and never-ending effort within the business. No longer is it acceptable or practical to just help people through a change from Point A to Point B. Technology is constantly changing. Access to data can reshape almost any component of the business. People are consistently looking to learn and improve. We are chasing higher levels of productivity, value, and innovation. Complacency sets in fast, so you need to develop a plan to deliver new types of services, support, and learning platforms that are in sync with the initiatives that are best for the people and the business.

Of course, it is not practical for you, the leader, to be in the trenches in perpetuity. However, you do need to have some level of optics into these efforts that are constantly supporting, training, communicating, and mentoring peoples' abilities to interact, grow, and be productive.

How can this be effective at your organization? This is quite a change from how businesses have traditionally supported employees. Simply providing access to break-fix help desks, pushing a ton of information out via email, offering classroom training, and many other legacy services for employees just don't cut it any longer. You need a small team that's solely dedicated to enabling employees to be as capable, engaged, and productive as possible. And it must be facilitated in a way that's in concert with your goals and objectives for the business as well as with the employees' careers and development. Keep in mind: This is not a concierge effort that provides fringe benefits. This is constantly understanding how your business can creatively and proactively provide resources that engage people through learning and ultimately support productivity.

TODAY

Identify your "Enablement Team." Think through your Strike Force members and any others that have risen to the occasion over the previous 27 days. Perhaps someone who was undecided and then partnered with you to inspire their team very effectively. The point of the exercise is to come up with three people in the organization who can see the big picture, effectively work among the silos that comprise much of the organization, and communicate and collaborate with you appropriately. This Enablement Team's work will pay dividends. The more they align people and interactions with outcomes, the higher the level of productivity at your business. Here are a few ideas that I've witnessed to be successful:

- » Create a hierarchy of skill paths that create a company-wide baseline of skills and then narrow in focus for specific departments, teams, or individuals.
- » The Enablement Team should coordinate the training and learning programs with IT, HR, and the Learning and Development Group.
- » Integrate Digital Adoption Platforms mentioned in Day 14 with any other Learning Management Systems that are in place.
- » Make sure that the Enablement Team meets with key business managers and leaders at least quarterly.
- » The Enablement Team should have an eye toward the future to maintain awareness of training for new systems and tools as well as for new opportunities and requirements to upskill employees for the new roles and disciplines that Big Data will undoubtedly bring to your organization.

Note: I'd like to stress something important here. Through much of your work over these 30 days, you are going to build, strengthen, and deepen your relationship with a valuable group of employees. This exposes you to people that can and should be mentored and possibly offered valuable positions in the future. The Enablement Team you are constructing today can be an immensely important experience for a future leader as you expose them to "big picture" thinking.

DAY 29: APPOINT THE "SURROGATE" AND CHALLENGE THE STATUS QUO

For the past 28 days, you've rededicated yourself to be the leader who energizes your business. You've challenged yourself to think differently about the business, the people, and your objectives. You've descended into the weeds to connect directly with your employees and truly understand a legitimate bottom-up perspective of working at the organization.

You've sat with leadership and key stakeholders and taken stock of how they approach their jobs and how it impacts the day-to-day operations. You've thought through technology's role in the organization and how people and the business must examine and implement tools and platforms going forward. Bottom line: When you cracked open this book and started to read, you discovered a chasm that will never allow you to revert to your prior mindset and approach to leadership.

While the work you've done entrenching yourself within the guts of the organization over the past month was absolutely necessary, it's not practical for you to remain in that zone. You must float back to the helm and renew your commitment to provide a new level of leadership to the entire firm.

DAY 29: APPOINT THE "SURROGATE" AND CHALLENGE THE STATUS QUO

TODAY

You have extremely important work to do as you think through the mechanics of continuing the work required to complete the recalibration of the business. And while it can't be you in the weeds, you do need strong and capable resources to pick up that work. And importantly, you'll need to develop a dashboard that allows you the appropriate optics into the ongoing efforts.

You must appoint a strong and capable person to be the "Surrogate" over the next 11 months to track the initiatives that you have implemented as well as the ones that inevitably will evolve as The Culture Project mindset permeates the organization. Obvious candidates to consider might be the Outsider on your Strike Force or a key manager who has exhibited thoughts, energy, and actions that are in lockstep with you and the work you've done over these 30 days.

With the Surrogate in place, here's your infrastructure moving forward through the next 11 months to support your efforts. Think through exactly how you want these valuable resources to function every month.

» **Strike Force:** Over the past month, you've relied on this team to help you expose current perspectives, support new thinking, and allow new voices to rise to your ears. This team should remain in place to help provide governance and direction. If there's been realization that a member is no longer a fit or has been repositioned into another important role at the firm, this is the time to add someone new to the Strike Force. It must be someone who has exhibited the mindset and energy necessary to collaborate with you, your Surrogate, and the rest of the team. Bringing in some new blood can be a great opportunity to spark new thoughts and ideas at this point.

» **Administrator:** You've relied on the Administrator to keep on track logistically, and it is extremely important to maintain schedule cadence. By maintaining the meeting cadence, this function provides urgency required for the team to complete the activities they've committed to. It would be great if the original Administrator stayed in place especially if they are the leader's executive assistant

» **Surrogate:** You'll need someone to track all initiatives and become that central figure that you trust to make sure that the efforts continue. Your work on Days 18, 19, and 20 gave you and your Strike Force a list of initiatives that need to be led forward over the next 11 months. While the Surrogate won't be the leader that you are, they must be viewed as your representative over the next 11 months. When people are being asked for an update or are being given specific direction by the Surrogate, employees must feel as though it's all being channeled by you through this very important role. This trusted person must be tracking all initiatives that were defined during those Days 18, 19, and 20. They must be able to update you and the Strike Force. They must come back to you when key stakeholders anywhere in the business are slowing down your efforts. You've designed a set of plays over these 30 days, and the Surrogate is your quarterback that you are relying on to execute.

» **Enablement Team:** On Day 28, you assembled the Enablement Team, which would be important to any and all initiatives by constantly helping employees be aware of what's expected of them, be trained and skilled to work appropriately, and then track and report progress. This group of people should be in lockstep with the Surrogate and have the appropriate access to the Strike Force and you on the right occasions.

DAY 30: STRIKE FORCE MEETINGS FOR THE NEXT 11 MONTHS

You've done it. You've built a ramp for the business to take flight and thrust itself toward a new course and trajectory. It's imperative that you set the cadence for the infrastructure discussed in Day 29 to meet and collaborate. As earlier noted, you cannot remain in the weeds. However, you do need to stay connected, be the ultimate sponsor and be ready, willing, and able to remove any barriers and distractions that are challenging the Strike Force, the Surrogate, and the Enablement Team. That's your role in this effort moving forward.

TODAY

Begin by working with the Administrator to establish the go-forward plan with both the Strike Force and the Surrogate. Set up two meetings per month with them. Create an agenda that allows for the Surrogate to update you and the Strike Force on all active initiatives. The Surrogate can also meet separately with the Enablement Team to get updates around advancing the awareness and know-how to all users. Feel good about the great work that you've done to remediate the legacy mindset that beset your business with friction and complacency. Celebrate with your team. As a leader, you should be thinking and talking in terms that are a match for your renewed energy and spirit to achieve the goals you strive for to improve productivity and business results. Success breeds the best environment for the culture that you are now demanding.

CONCLUSION

Digital Transformation. There, I said it. People always want to label things. And, of course, it's only natural to further define them by applying acceptable standards à la best practices, unit costs, industry standards, etc. If I had authored this book to be one of the many in a parade of Digital Transformation tomes, those acceptable standards would have sucked out the ingenuity, practicality, and significance associated with the role that culture plays in any organization's journey to be a more sophisticated and modern business.

As well, it would have defined and positioned a set of prescribed digital fixes that, right out of the gate, would have had executive leadership reflexively delegating this "technical" and "digital" work to others within the firm and/or to a large consulting firm with the PowerPoint prowess to illustrate a corporate résumé brimming with experience for applying acceptable standards. As an entrepreneur, it is simply not in my DNA to join any parade of acceptable standards.

The ethos of this book is just as much about developing a leader's perspective as it is about developing an organization's culture. It's wholly ineffective for these two factors to be mutually exclusive. As the centuries old proverb says: "When a fish stinks, it stinks from the head all the way to the tail." The Culture Project asserts that this applies to a leader's approach to evolving technologies, enabling people and readying a business for the future. And while the obvious and immediate premise of this book is aligning talent and technology as the vehicle for better communication, collaboration, and productivity, the longer view is that these 30 days of work will instill a healthy and robust foundation inherently capable of spawning new businesses, new products and services, talented and innovative leaders, and the attributes a business needs to adopt in order to be relevant five or 10 years from now.

All that being said, it begs the question "What's next?" After the 30 days of The Culture Project, your team (the Surrogate, the Strike Force, the Enablement Team) will continue to follow through with the ideas and initiatives that have shaped your plan moving forward. What you can do as a leader is continue to grow and learn so that your perspective is one that can continuously add value, identify opportunities, or perhaps just better understand strategic initiatives that are presented to you going forward. Here are a few of my favorite suggestions for continuing to enhance your leadership.

Attend one or two conferences each year that focus on the future of technology. One of my favorites is Emtech, the annual *MIT Technology Review*'s conference on emerging technology and trends

Read books that help you understand the future landscape of business. I recommend *Competing in the Age of AI: Strategy and Leadership When Algorithms and Networks Run the World* by Marco Iansiti and Karim R. Lakhani. The authors do a wonderful job of educating readers about the power of technology by walking through real-world cases from some of the world's most amazing businesses. And while the game-changing results are often highlighted within "newer" technology driven businesses, it shows us the path forward in that all businesses will need to leverage Artificial Intelligence and Automation to compete and thrive.

Continuously seek out and understand new businesses and new business models. Not only is this valuable to inform your organization's current practices; but it also informs you of new vendors and partners that can have a positive impact on all areas of your organization. There are countless startups and venture capital–backed businesses that represent cutting-edge (or bleeding-edge) businesses and business models. Here are a few that I recommend looking into.

- » Uptake Technologies and founder/CEO Brad Keywell are on the forefront of AI software for heavy industry by turning data into actionable insights for optimizing asset performance (uptake.com).
- » WalkMe—led by co-founders, CEO Dan Adika and President Rafi Sweary—is revolutionizing the training industry and providing groundbreaking solutions

> that enable true user adoption and upskilling for the workforce (walkme.com).

» Lemonade, Inc., and its co-founders, CEO Daniel Schreiber and President/COO Shai Wininger, are challenging the traditional insurance industry model by charging flat fees and donating the remainder of premiums to charity rather than keeping 100 percent of the underwriting profit (lemonade.com).

It's my hope that The Culture Project has awakened something in you that provides the energy, curiosity, and, most of all, the guts to see where you can take your organization. While there undoubtedly will be hard work and uncomfortable conversations (guts!), it will be extremely rewarding to lead, grow, and influence a business, a workplace, and a special team of people to remove barriers and create a spectacular future.

I wish you luck.

READING LIST

Zaffron, Steve & Logan, Dave. *The Three Laws of Performance: Rewriting the Future of Your Organization and Your Life* (2011)
https://threelawsofperformance.com/
https://www.wiley.com/en-us/The+Three+Laws+of
+Performance%3A+Rewriting+the+Future+of+Your
+Organization+and+Your+Life-p-9781118043127

Dweck, Carol S. *Mindset: The New Psychology of Success* (2012)
https://www.penguinrandomhouse.com/books/44330/
mindset-by-carol-s-dweck-phd/

Cuddy, Amy. *Presence: Bringing Your Boldest Self to Your Biggest Challenges* (2016)
https://www.littlebrown.com/titles/amy-cuddy/presence/9780316256575/

Ravasi, D. & Schultz, M. *Responding to Organizational Identity Threats: Exploring the Role of Organizational Culture* (2006)
https://journals.aom.org/doi/10.5465/amj.2006.21794663

Iansiti, M & Lakhani, K. *Competing in the Age of AI: Strategy and Leadership When Algorithms and Networks Run the World* (2020)
https://store.hbr.org/product/competing-in-the-age-of-ai-strategy-and-leadership-when-algorithms-and-networks-run-the-world/10272

ACKNOWLEDGMENTS

I want to thank everyone that played a role in shaping the perspective and advice that I put forth in The Culture Project. This includes many amazing clients as well as advisors and colleagues including Mark Stevens, Sandy Diehl, Tod Lickerman, Tom Santiago, Tony Tata, Bryan Berthold, Stefan Dietrich, Sheila Refael, Traci Potenza, Adam Bunk, Eliza Packard, and Evan Avidane.

Special thanks to Jeff Gothelf and Josh Seiden at Sense & Respond Press for your guidance and patience.

And thank you to my family—Dawn, Sophie, Tommy, Amelia, and Luke—for giving me the space and courage to write this book. I can't wait to see where our journey leads us next.

THOMAS BRADBURY is a career-long entrepreneur having successfully exited two consulting businesses that focused on technology selection and implementation for corporate clients traversing transformational workplace projects. After performing dozens of workplace technology assessments for renowned corporate brands as well as vital middle-market businesses across North America, Bradbury wrote *The Culture Project* to motivate business owners and senior executives to address the most basic and fundamental issues that hold back their respective organizations from establishing a culture that truly allows for the alignment of talent and technology. With the belief that this type of culture will determine success over the next decade, Bradbury recently started his next venture, Helix2, which continues to consult business owners and senior business executives as well as provide advisory services to the technology services companies that these end user organizations rely on for advice, services, and support.

Tom@helix2.us
www.helix2.us
thomasbradbury

Made in the USA
Monee, IL
11 December 2021